# Getting To Know...

# Nature's Children

# GORILLAS

## Merebeth Switzer

SCHOLASTIC INC.

New York  Toronto  London  Auckland  Sydney
Mexico City  New Delhi  Hong Kong  Buenos Aires

# FACTS IN BRIEF

**Classification of the gorilla**
Class: *Mammalia* (mammals)
Order: *Primates* (apes, monkeys, lemurs, people)
Family: *Pongidae* (people-like apes)
Genus: *Gorilla*
Species: *Gorilla gorilla*

**World distribution.** Africa.

**Habitat.** Forest and mountain forest.

**Distinctive physical characteristics.** The largest of the apes, gorillas have small ears, eyes deep under heavy brow ridges, a large jaw, and arms that are longer than their legs.

**Habits.** Live on the ground, only females and young climb in trees at all; live in small family groups, active during the day, sleep in nests, newly made each night. Males will roar and beat on their chests to frighten off intruders.

**Diet.** Fruit and vegetation.

Published by Scholastic Inc.
90 Old Sherman Turnpike, Danbury, Connecticut 06816.

SCHOLASTIC and associated logos are trademarks of Scholastic Inc.

ISBN 0-7172-6693-1

Printed in the U.S.A.

## Have you ever wondered . . .

High up in the misty mountains of central Africa a large dark figure squats quietly beside a fallen tree. He lifts his head up and his large nostrils pull in the smells of the forests. The smell tells him he is not alone. Soon he hears the swooshing of branches, the thumping of bare feet on the dirt and quiet low mutterings.

The bushes part and a much larger gorilla steps into the clearing. He stares at the young male and then reaches out to grasp the branch of a small tree. With a grunt he breaks it off and begins to nibble on the tough stalk.

The meeting is peaceful enough. Can these be the creatures that inspired the stories of the fierce jungle ape, King Kong? Let's take a closer look and find out more about the famous but secretive gorilla.

# A Jungle Family

The big male gorilla is not alone—other heads bob among the shrubs. Several females and youngsters have joined him. One mother carries a small baby clasped to her massive chest.

A playful youngster charges the male. In a flying tackle she lands on his back. He calmly continues to eat but his huge hand reaches up and pulls off the offender, dumping her on the ground in an awkward somersault.

The youngster attacks again, this time grasping the adult's left leg. Clinging with all fours, she takes a playful bite. The male gives a warning growl, and when she persists, a quick nip. The youngster scuttles away to the safety of her mother.

*The average gorilla family consists of 5 to 10 members.*

# Gorillas and Their Relatives

Gorillas are the biggest members of a group of animals known as primates. The group is a large one and includes the other great apes (chimpanzees and orangutans) and the lesser apes (gibbons and siamangs) as well as baboons and monkeys—and humans.

While there is only one species of gorilla, there are three different types: the Eastern and Western Lowland Gorillas and the Mountain Gorilla. Although these three have much in common, they do not look alike nor do they always behave in the same ways.

Opposite page: *The orangutan weighs about the same as an average human adult male—around 70-90 kilograms (150-200 pounds).*

Mountain Gorilla
Eastern Lowland Gorilla
Western Lowland Gorilla

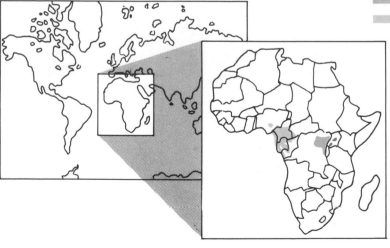

*The shaded area on this map show where gorillas live in Africa.*

## The Mountain Gorilla

The Mountain Gorilla is the largest and the rarest of the gorillas. It is very dark in color, and because it lives up in the mountains where temperatures can be low, it has longer hair than the lowland gorillas. It also has larger jaws and teeth. But because individual gorillas can look quite different from one another, telling the types apart is sometimes difficult for a non-specialist.

The Mountain Gorilla is found high up in the volcanic mountains of Virunga on the Zaire-Rwanda-Uganda border in eastern central Africa.

*The Mountain Gorilla has shorter arms, slightly shorter legs and broader hands and feet than the Lowland Gorilla.*

# The Lowland Gorillas

The Lowland Gorillas are found, as their name suggests, in lush lowlands or plateaus.

The Eastern Lowland Gorilla lives in the same region as the Mountain Gorilla. It has black hair like its mountain cousins, but both Lowland Gorillas have a distinct ridge over the top of the nose. The Mountain Gorilla does not have this ridge, and this part of its face therefore appears smoother.

The Western Lowland Gorilla lives nearly 1600 kilometres (1000 miles) away from its eastern cousins, near the west coast of the continent. Its coat is gray-brown and the hair on its head may have tinges of red.

*The hair of the Lowland Gorilla is somewhat shorter than that of the Mountain Gorilla.*

## That Special Walk

With their long, powerful arms, gorillas are well suited to their life in the jungle. Although they *can* walk upright, they rarely do, preferring to move through the forest on all fours. However, the fact that their arms are so much longer than their legs gives them a semi-upright stance as they lope along in their characteristic half-walk, half-trot.

Like other apes, gorillas walk on the soles of their feet but not on their palms. Instead, they curl up their fingers and support themselves on their knuckles—which, as a result, become quite calloused.

Because of their size and weight, most adult gorillas stay on the ground, but young ones spend a lot of time in the trees. Some of the lighter adults also climb trees to look for food, swinging from one to another by their arms.

*Try to knuckle walk like a gorilla and you will soon discover why its arms have to be longer than yours.*

## Suitable Senses

Like people, gorillas have their eyes at the front of their face. Because of this, they can judge distance well, and it is thought that they also see colors. This may help them decide what to eat, although they seem to some extent to go by their sense of smell as well. A gorilla will often take the time to thoroughly sniff any food it has doubts about.

A gorilla has two small, human-like ears on either side of its head and probably hears better than you do. This is important in the dense jungle where it is often impossible to see more than an arm's length away.

*It's not easy to sneak up on a gorilla, but who would want to anyway?*

# The Silverback

Male and female gorillas look alike until they reach about 8 to 12 years of age. At this point, silver-gray hairs begin to grow on the shoulders, back and flanks of the male's body. He puts on more weight and develops larger muscles as he becomes an adult. Because of the silver hairs on his back, he is known as a "silverback."

The silverback's head is massive, with a crest of bone in the center of his skull. This gives him a high forehead that makes him look different than younger males and all females.

Despite the stories of giant gorillas, the largest silverback reaches only about 170 centimetres (5 1/2 feet) in height, although he may tip the scales at 200 kilograms (450 pounds)! That's about three times the weight of a man of the same height. Female gorillas are shorter than males and may weigh only half as much.

*Silverback Mountain Gorilla.*

## Living Together

Gorillas live in family groups called troops. These troops vary in size. They may have one silverback, a few females and their young, and sometimes a few young males known as "blackbacks." However, some troops have 20 animals or more.

The silverback is in charge of the group. He leads the troop, challenges intruders and scouts out new feeding areas to check for any danger.

Many animals refuse to share any part of their territory with others of their species. The territories of gorilla troops, however, often overlap. In fact, it is not unusual for two or more troops to live side by side quite peacefully, sharing feeding grounds and rest areas—and even spending short periods of time together.

*A family affair.*

## Getting the Message Across

Gorillas have many ways of communicating with one another and the rest of the world. They are fairly quiet animals, but they can produce quite a range of grunts, lip-smacks, huffs and other sounds when they want to.

They also use their faces to show how they feel: a tired gorilla yawns, a baby smiles and giggles when tickled, and a nervous gorilla may bite its lower lip. And an angry gorilla can make a face so ferocious that that alone should be enough to strike fear in the heart of an intruder.

Anyone who has seen the terrifying display of a silverback finds it hard to imagine one living in peaceful harmony even with its own kind. But the performance is simply a way of scaring away other animals. And it works. After the complex display of screaming, ground bashing, chest thumping and teeth gnashing, the silverback will usually take his challenge no farther. Of course, he usually doesn't have to. Few creatures are foolhardy enough to call his bluff.

Opposite page: *"Come closer. I dare you!"*

# Thundering Thumps

All gorillas thump their chests. Even youngsters do it, mainly, it seems, when they want someone to play with them.

Even among adults, chest beating sometimes seems to be done simply for pleasure, rather like a loud cheer on the last day of school. At other times, it may be a sign of frustration. One captive gorilla was known to do it whenever she had trouble completing a task she was working on.

The sound of a silverback thumping his chest to let others know his troop is feeding in the area is particularly impressive. Small chambers in his giant chest make the sound louder, and the resounding booms act like a loud shout: "I'm here and I'm strong."

*In the wild, gorillas may live for 35 years.*

## Moseying Along

The gorillas' day starts at dawn, which is always around six in the morning near the equator where they live. One by one the gorillas awaken and get up from their night nests. A lucky one or two may simply be able to pull over a vine and enjoy breakfast in bed.

Soon, however, the troop moves on at a leisurely pace to search farther afield for food. A troop's home range may cover from 5 to 30 square kilometres (2 to 12 square miles), and gorillas are careful never to strip a feeding area bare. So they move every day. Some days they do not go very far, perhaps only the length of a city block. On other days they may cover greater distances, but they seldom travel much more than a kilometre (half a mile) in one day. Only very rarely will they move outside of their home range.

*Traveling in style.*

# Eating

Eating takes up most of a gorilla's waking hours. Gorillas are herbivores, or plant-eaters, and they eat mainly leaves, twigs, barks and grasses. These are relatively low in nutrients and high in fiber, and so they must eat vast amounts—up to 14 kilograms (30 pounds) per day in order to remain healthy.

Gorillas do not seem to have the same taste in food as we do. They are particularly fond of bitter or acid, vinegary tasting foods. And they often show a definite preference for what would seem to us to be the least appetizing part of any given plant. Can you imagine gnawing on a twig of an apple tree rather than munching on a crisp, sweet apple? A gorilla would choose the twig almost every time! And it would as soon—if not sooner—eat tough bark rather than fresh green shoots.

You have probably heard people say, "There's no accounting for tastes," and this certainly seems to be true in the case of gorillas. They will eat lots of different foods, but they definitely have their favorites.

Opposite page: *Gorillas get much of the water they need from the plants they eat.*

## Nap-Time and Bath-Time

Naps are an important part of the gorillas' day. Since they start feeding so early in the morning, they are usually ready to settle down for their midday siesta about ten o'clock. Usually they sleep until about two in the afternoon. This works out very well because these are the hours when the tropical sun is at its hottest and its intense rays are best avoided.

The long naps probably also help the gorillas digest the large amount of food they ate in the morning so that they wake up not only refreshed but ready to feed some more.

The weather in the tropics where gorillas live is very humid, and it sometimes rains almost every day. Gorillas do not seem to head for shelter when a rainstorm hits. They simply stop what they are doing and sit quite cheerfully in the rain. Their thick fur may offer some protection, but they often must receive a thorough soaking—which doesn't appear to bother them at all.

It is surprising that although gorillas don't mind being wet, they will not swim if they can avoid it.

Opposite page:
*Laid back
Lowland.*

## Night Nests

Gorillas settle down for the night at sunset. Given their long midday snooze, this no doubt makes it seem that they spend a great deal of their time sleeping—and they do, as much as 16 hours each day.

They don't have a permanent home they return to at night. Instead, when evening approaches, they just find a suitable spot near the feeding place their day's wanderings have taken them to. There, each gorilla collects branches and vines and weaves them together to fashion its own sleeping nest. Very young gorillas are spared this chore as they share their mothers' nests.

Scientists can tell the number of gorillas in a troop and estimate their size by counting and studying the empty nests they find each morning.

*Gorillas do not defend their territory the way many other animals do.*

## Few Fears

Gorillas are peaceful creatures. They mind their own business and other animals usually don't bother them. In fact, adult gorillas have almost no enemies. The young are vulnerable and occasionally one may be taken by a leopard, but this is uncommon since gorillas live together in family groups. The young are normally well protected by their parents and aunts and uncles.

The greatest natural threat to gorillas appears to be sickness and injuries. Gorillas suffer from many of the same diseases and get injured in many of the same ways we do.

*This young gorilla should have watched where it was walking.*

# Mating

Gorillas can mate at any time of year. In established troops, it is usually only the silverback leader that fathers the babies. A younger male will occasionally mate with one of the females, but it is more usual for him to set out on his own and try to lure a young female away from another troop.

When males compete for a female, they will try to scare each other off with elaborate threat displays and they may actually fight. The female usually chooses to go with the one who seems the strongest and therefore the best able to protect her babies from danger.

*The Mountain Gorilla is rarer than the Lowland and is considered an endangered species.*

## Meet the Baby

The female gorilla gives birth about nine months after mating. She usually has just one baby, though occasional cases of twins have been recorded.

A newborn gorilla looks rather like a human baby, but it weighs less—just a little under or over 2 kilograms (4 to 5 pounds). Its skin is pink with grayish tinges, and it has little hair except for a mass on top of its head and a white tuft on its rump. Its hair grows in quickly, however, and before long the baby is well covered with fur except on its chest and tummy. The white tuft will eventually disappear, though not entirely until the youngster is almost four years old.

*Young gorillas are always near their mother's side.*

## Quick Learners

When you were little, your mother had to take care of you. You had to learn how to roll over, crawl, sit up, stand up and finally, when you were about a year old, to walk. A baby gorilla is just the same, though it progresses a little faster.

For the first few weeks, it spends most of its time nursing in its mother's arms. At about three months it can crawl and normally it is walking well before it is nine months old.

Like almost all babies—animal *and* human—young gorillas are both playful and curious. As soon as they can crawl they eagerly begin exploring the world around them. And they have probably learned to climb by the time they can walk.

*This 6-month-old gorilla still has a lot to learn before it is ready to live on its own.*

## A Sharing Family

If you have younger brothers and sisters, you probably play with them and do your best to help your parents take care of them. Gorilla families are the same. All the gorillas in the troop take turns at watching over and caring for the baby or at least amusing it. In this way young gorillas learn what they will need to know in order to someday care for their own babies.

The little one enjoys all the loving attention it gets from other family members, but for two or three years it will always head straight back to mom when it is hungry or when danger threatens. By the time it is four, it is ready to be fairly independent—which is just as well since by then there will probably be a new baby claiming mom's attention. The youngster still has a lot of growing up to do, however, and it will be several more years before it is ready to start a family of its own.

*Hitching a ride.*

## Learning About Gorillas

Although many special reserves exist for them, gorillas are becoming rarer. Like many animals, they are threatened by the growth of the human population. Each day people are moving closer to their jungle home, clearing land for farming and for fuel and timber. As the forests disappear, so does the gorilla's food supply.

Much has been learned in recent years about the ways and needs of these remarkable animals. The better we all understand them, the more hope there is that the efforts now being made to preserve their wilderness home will be successful.

# Words to Know

**Blackback**   A young male gorilla.

**Callous**   A tough pad of built-up skin.

**Herbivore**   A plant-eating animal.

**Mate**   To come together to produce young. Either member of an animal pair is also the other's mate.

**Plateau**   High flat land.

**Primate**   An animal which belongs to the order *Primates,* such as a gorilla, monkey or human being.

**Reserve**   An area where wildlife is protected by law.

**Silverback**   A mature male gorilla.

**Troop**   A group of gorillas that lives together.

# INDEX

**Cover Photo:** Ron Garrison (Zoological Society of San Diego)

**Photo Credits:** Nancy Adams (EPI), pages 4, 24, 27; Boyd Norton, pages 7, 11, 23, 32-33, 39, 43; Bill Ivy, pages 8, 36; John Cancalosi, pages 12, 16; Ron Garrison (Zoological Society of San Diego), pages 15, 44; Peter Drowne/E.R. Degginger, pages 19, 20; Zoological Society of San Diego, page 28; Metro Toronto Zoo, page 31; Kjell B. Sandved, page 35; Columbus Zoo, page 40.

# Getting To Know...

# Nature's Children

# ANTS

Caroline Greenland

SCHOLASTIC INC.

New York   Toronto   London   Auckland   Sydney
Mexico City   New Delhi   Hong Kong   Buenos Aires

# Facts in Brief

**Classification of North American ants**

Class:     *Insecta* (insects)
Order:    *Hymenoptera* (bees, wasps, and ants)
Family:  *Formicidae* (ant family)
Genus:   60 genera exist in North America, comprising hundreds of species

**World distribution.**  Closely related species are found in most places in the world.

**Habitat.**  Varies with species.

**Distinctive physical characteristics.**  Large head and slender mid-section; two antennae; some have a stinger at the tip of the abdomen.

**Habits.**  Lives in organized colonies; most species build nests.

**Diet.**  Varies with species.

Revised edition copyright © 2000 by Scholastic Inc.
Original material © 1985 Grolier Limited.
All rights reserved.

Published by Scholastic Inc.
90 Old Sherman Turnpike, Danbury, Connecticut  06816.

SCHOLASTIC and associated logos are trademarks of Scholastic Inc.

ISBN 0-7172-6693-1

Printed in the U.S.A.

*Edited by:* Elizabeth Grace Zuraw
*Photo Rights*: Ivy Images

*Photo Editor:* Nancy Norton
*Cover Design*: Niemand Design

## Have you ever wondered . . .

The next time you have a picnic, see how long it takes you to spot an ant. Chances are that one of these remarkable little insects will be crawling over your tablecloth in a matter of minutes. Ants have an uncanny ability to find you and your food in record time, don't they?

And that's not the only amazing thing about ants. They have incredible determination to survive in the face of huge obstacles. Imagine coming out of your home each day and pushing your way through a thick forest and then scaling the Empire State Building or the Sears Tower. Translated into ant terms, that's exactly what an ant does when it runs through a "forest" of grass and then up a plant stem or branch.

Ants are also surprisingly strong. They can carry up to 27 times their own weight, and not even puff! But perhaps the most amazing thing about ants is the way they cooperate with each other for the good of the whole ant *colony,* or group. It's this tremendous cooperation that makes ants some of the most interesting creatures in the animal world.

## Ants Everywhere

Do you have ants in your backyard or in your house? Most likely you do. No matter where you live in North America—in rainy coastal areas or in a desert, on a mountain or in a forest—ants are there.

Ants have lived on Earth for millions of years. Long ago they were found only in the hot tropical areas of the world. But today there are ants everywhere, except in extremely cold arctic lands.

In all, there are more than 35,000 kinds of ants in the world. Some are as large as a new eraser—up to 2.5 inches (more than 6 centimeters) long. Others are so small that they're difficult to see.

Ants come in a range of colors, too. They can be brown, yellow, red, or black—but black ants are the most common.

*Every ant in a colony has a job to do. These red ants are working in the nursery, tending to the larvae that one day soon will be the colony's newest members.*

## Ants Are Insects

All ants are part of a much bigger animal group—namely, insects. Within this large group, their closest relatives are wasps and bees. In fact, some wasps look very much like ants!

Like all adult insects, ants have six legs and three separate parts to their bodies. The first part is the head, which has two feelers called *antennae* (an-TEN-ee). The middle section is the *thorax* (THAW-racks). The tail or last part is the *abdomen* (AB-duh-men).

The next time you see a creepy-crawly, give it the insect test. Count the legs and body parts. Is it an insect? If it doesn't have the right number of legs and correct kinds of body parts, you may be looking at a spider or a centipede instead!

Also like other insects, an ant doesn't have lungs. It takes in air through small holes called *spiracles* (SPEER-uh-culls) along the sides of its thorax and abdomen. The air passes into small breathing tubes that branch through all parts of the ant's body.

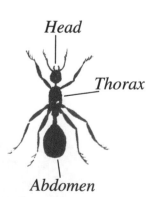

*Head*

*Thorax*

*Abdomen*

## A Life Full of Changes

An ant passes the insect test with flying colors. But ants don't always look like the six-legged creatures we usually see in our gardens. During their lives, they go through several changes. This process of change is called *metamorphosis*. At different stages during its metamorphosis, an ant looks very un-ant-like.

Ants start life as tiny white eggs. Out of these hatch worm-like grubs called *larvae* (LAR-vee). Each larva (LAR-vuh) spins itself a *cocoon,* or covering, in which it undergoes even more changes. At this cocoon stage, the ant-to-be is called a *pupa* (PYOO-puh). While inside the cocoon, the pupa develops legs, antennae, and all the other necessary body parts. Finally, the pupa is ready to emerge from its cocoon as an adult ant, looking the way we expect an ant to look.

As soon as the new ant breaks out of its cocoon, it's ready to take its place in the ant colony.

## Ant Armor

An ant is entirely covered by a hard, tough overcoat that's just like armor. Knights of old had to put on armor for protection, but an ant's armor, or *exoskeleton,* is built in.

The ant's exoskeleton is made up of a hard material called *chitin.* This material is very much like the substance your fingernails are made of. And just as the bones of your skeleton give you shape, an ant's exoskeleton gives it shape, too.

*Your skeleton is inside your body, but an ant's skeleton, its exoskeleton, is on the outside of its body.*

## Ant Antennae

Opposite page:
*Like this carpenter ant, all ants have elbowed antennae.*

The next time you see an ant, watch how it moves its antennae. You may see the ant wave them in the wind or tap them on the ground all around itself. What is the ant doing? It may be smelling for food, testing for wetness, feeling for vibrations, or even taking the temperature! As you've probably guessed, its antennae give an ant the information it needs about the world.

If you could look at an antenna under a microscope, you'd see rows of tiny bumps up and down its length. These bumps pick up scents—so the ant can actually smell with its antennae. By touching something with its feelers, an ant can thoroughly inspect its food or feel its way through the maze of tunnels that make up its home. The ant, however, doesn't have good vision. But then, good sight isn't so necessary if you've got a pair of antennae, is it?

You can tell that its feelers are important to the ant by the care it gives them. An ant constantly cleans them with its mouth and legs. In fact, an ant even has a special built-in "brush" of hairs on each of its front legs for this very purpose.

*The tiny hairs that cover an ant's body enable it to feel its surroundings.*

## Warning System

An ant's antennae act as danger detectors by picking up vibrations from the ground. If an ant senses strange vibrations, it can scoot off, out of harm's way. This makes sneaking up on an ant difficult.

For extra safety, the ant has a back-up warning system. It has hair-like spikes all over its exoskeleton. These "hairs" come out through the tough outer shell and are attached to nerves under the surface of the exoskeleton. When anything—even a breeze—touches the hairs, the ant takes note. If it thinks an enemy is near, away it runs to safety.

## Neat Feet

Have you ever wondered how an ant can walk on a ceiling and not fall off? It's simple. Each of the ant's six legs has five flexible segments and ends with a pair of tiny claws. When an ant walks up or down something like a wall, or across a surface upside down, the tiny claws hook themselves into cracks and bumps. There are very few surfaces that are too smooth for an ant to walk on. Even something like glass, which appears perfectly smooth to us, has ripples and crevices large enough for an ant's claws to grab onto.

## Machine Mouth

You use your mouth mainly for talking and eating. Ants' mouths are different. They're simply holes in the front of their heads! Instead of having lips and jaws like yours, an ant has hard pieces of exoskeleton at the edges of its mouth. These pieces, called *mandibles,* swing together like pairs of tongs to close the hole. An ant's mandibles have many uses. Some ants use them as weapons or as tools for carving out tunnels through earth or into wood. Ants also use them for carrying eggs and larvae in their nests and for moving other objects. In fact, ants use their mandibles the way you use your arms.

And, of course, an ant uses its mouth and mandibles for eating, too. An ant also has a tongue, but it doesn't have teeth. After all, who needs teeth when they've got jaws so strong that they can be used to cut and bite and hold onto things?

## Storage Stomachs

Ants have to share their food. And what better way to carry it back to the colony than in their stomachs? Ants have two-part stomachs. In one part, food for the colony is temporarily stored. This stomach is called the *crop*. In the other part, the ant keeps its own personal supply of food.

When an ant finds food, it chews it up and dissolves it into a liquid. Most of this liquid food goes into the crop, and a very small bit goes into the other part of the stomach for the ant's own use.

Back at the colony, the ant with the full crop helps feed the other ants. Now that's sharing!

*Some ants collect the sweet-tasting liquid that oozes from the tiny aphid. Such ants are called dairy ants because they "herd" the aphids together and then "milk" them by gently stroking them. Dairy ants live in the little sandy mounds commonly seen along paths.*

## Colony Life

One ant by itself wouldn't live very long. Perhaps that's why you rarely see a single ant. There's always another one close by. And another. And another. But it's not their numbers that make ants different from other insects—it's their organization. Ants live in colonies that vary in size from a dozen to thousands upon thousands of ants. Within these colonies, ants cooperate with each other, much the same as people do in cities or towns.

In most colonies, there are three different *castes,* or types, of ants. Each caste looks different from the others and makes a different contribution to the colony.

*Size comparison*

*Worker*          *Male*          *Queen*

The first caste is made up of queen ants. There's usually only one queen per colony. The queen is larger than the other ants and, for the first part of her life, she has wings. Her job is twofold. First, she is responsible for founding a new colony, and secondly, she must lay the eggs to produce new ants that will keep the colony going.

The second caste is made up of winged male ants. They have only one job to perform in their very short lives—they must *mate* with the queen—come together with her in order to produce young. After mating, the males die.

The third caste is made up of the female worker ants. Some of their jobs are to clean the nest, dig and maintain tunnels, tend to the nursery, get food, and protect the nest from enemies. Worker ants are the ones you most commonly see. The survival of the colony ultimately rests on their shoulders, although it is the queen that begins the whole process and provides the eggs that make the continuation of the colony possible.

slave raiders carrying off young

tending pupae

guest fly larvae

mutual feeding

tending larvae

a beetle guest

tending a queen

nest of thief ants

gathering honeydew from aphids

bringing in food

digging new tunnels

resting and grooming

This illustration shows some of the activities inside the underground nest of a common ant. The colony's life centers on the queen, who is constantly fed and cleaned by workers. They also carry off the eggs she lays to chambers where they hatch into larvae. The larvae, and later the pupae, are continually cleaned and fed by nursery ants. In the nest there may also be "guest" insects—though they're not invited. Usually they're intruders who move in to take advantage of the ants' comfortable quarters.

While some workers do housekeeping and nursery chores, others have the job of finding food and bringing it back to the nest. And workers called soldiers defend the colony from enemies, including slave-making ants from other colonies. These raiders steal eggs that will develop into future workers for their own colony.

## Mating Flight

Imagine sitting outdoors on a warm summer evening. Suddenly the air around you is filled with flying ants. What you're witnessing is the mating flight of ants. That mating flight marks the beginning of new ant colonies.

In one gigantic whirring insect cloud, the young queens and the male ants fly high above the ground to mate. After an hour or so, they fall back down to the ground. The males' brief but vital task is accomplished. Soon they will die, but the lifetime work of the queens is just beginning.

*In winter, ants that live in cold regions move to the deepest part of their nests. In the spring they come out again, sometimes in large masses, to take in the rays of the newly warming sun.*

## All Hail the Queen

The queen must find a suitable place for her colony-to-be. As soon as she does, her wings fall off. She no longer needs them.

Next the queen busies herself by tunneling underground to make a nest. All alone, she seals herself into her tunnel and starts to lay eggs.

Now comes a long time of waiting in isolation, sometimes for as long as nine months. During this period, the queen tends her eggs carefully. Once they've hatched, she feeds the larvae with her own saliva, which has food value. But how does the queen feed herself? Believe it or not, she absorbs her now-useless wing muscles for food and occasionally eats a few of the smaller eggs.

*The queen ant is the mother of the colony.*
*She may live up to 15 years.*

## Hatch Time

Once the ants have hatched and undergone their metamorphosis from grub-like larvae to adult ants, they're ready to help their queen set up a colony. Now the queen can settle back and receive the royal treatment that queens customarily enjoy. She'll be completely taken care of so that she can be free to carry out her main task for the colony—laying eggs.

One of the workers' most important tasks is finding food. Some go out immediately. Soon they return and pass the food they've gathered to the queen and then to the larvae. Other workers clean the eggs and care for the new larvae and pupae. Meanwhile, still other workers busily dig new tunnels to enlarge the new colony's nest.

*Ant larvae are white and look like little caterpillars. Nursery workers carefully clean and feed them.*

## Home, Sweet Home

You may have seen many ant homes and never given them a second thought. Remember those small mounds of earth, bare of grass and with lots of holes poked into the top surface? If you saw ants scurrying in and out of these holes, you probably were looking at an ant home.

Many North American ants live in nests that go deep underground. Above ground some of these nests look like miniature mountains. But below ground is a complicated system of tunnels and rooms—what amounts to a whole city, in fact!

Depending upon the type of ant, there may be storerooms for food. There will be nursery chambers where workers care for the eggs, larvae, and pupae. There might even be a series of empty rooms where the young can be moved in case the nest is damaged or attacked. And, of course, there's the royal suite, where the queen lives.

The ground isn't the only place for an ant home. Can you guess where a carpenter ant lives? That's right, in wood. They can be found in dead logs and stumps, or if you're really unlucky, even in your house. If you find little piles of sawdust under a hole in a piece of wood, chances are you have carpenter ants living with you.

Other ants build simple homes high up in trees or under rocks, while still others burrow under tree roots and dig out elaborate dwellings.

*Some ant larvae spin silk cocoons around themselves. The silk is made of saliva from their mouths. Inside the cocoons, the would-be ants change into adults.*

# Chemical Kisses

How do the thousands of ants in a colony know what to do and when to do it? In their own special way, they're actually taking orders from the queen. She's constantly giving off chemical substances called *pheromones* (FEH-ruh-mones) that are passed on to her workers as they clean her. Then these ants pass on the substances to other ants by a sort of kiss and by touching antennae.

All the other ants produce pheromones of their own, too. When an ant touches another ant's mouth and antennae, the ant picks up chemicals that transmit a lot of different information. It can tell if the other ant is from its home colony, what it's been eating, and what job the ant has. In short, these "kisses" are the ants' way of binding the colony together.

Even when an ant is in the egg or pupal stage, it communicates by giving off chemical messages. At this time, the message is likely to be, "Get me out of here." Nursery workers get this signal and rush to help the egg or pupa, tearing its case to let the larva or adult out.

Opposite page: *When ants "kiss" and tap each other with their antennae, they're "talking" to each other. That kind of communication is what holds a colony together, enabling it to survive.*

*To an ant, there's no such word as "can't." Moths and
butterflies many times the ant's size are fair game.*

## Finding Food

Being able to find food is essential to every living creature, and ants are no exception. Here, too, these little insects are good at helping each other for the benefit of the whole colony. For instance, if one leaf-cutting ant returns to the nest with a leaf from a lush patch of plants, the ant immediately communicates this information to the other workers.

She does this by running about, striking the workers with her antennae. Her message is, "Hurry up!" For as she was returning to the nest, she had left a pheromone scent trail all the way from the plants to the nest. She knows that the scent trail lasts for only a few minutes. If the other ants hurry, they'll be able to back-track along her trail before it disappears. And then they, too, will be able to take advantage of the good new food source.

## Farming Ants

Opposite page:
*Leaf-cutter ants snip off pieces of leaves, grasp them in their mandibles, and then travel in long lines back and forth to their colony.*

As much as ants enjoy the treats you take along on a picnic, they're far from dependent on you and your picnic basket for food.

Some ants are farmers. The leaf-cutting ants of Louisiana and Texas take leaves into their underground nests and grow a special *fungus,* or kind of mushroom, on them. The fungus thrives in the darkness of the nest and the ants eat it whenever they're hungry. This means that the ants have to leave the safety of their nests only when they need more leaves.

Still other ants are "dairy farmers." They tend aphids the way dairy farmers tend cows. Aphids, tiny insects that feed on plant juices, suck up more juice than they need. Ants take advantage of the surplus. They gently stroke the backs of the aphids with their antennae, causing the aphids to discharge tiny drops of honeydew. The ants then store the honeydew in their crops. It's a convenient arrangement. The ant gets the sweet food for its colony, and the aphid is protected from other insects by having the ants around.

## Different Tastes

Carpenter ants have different tastes. Although these large dark ants spend their lives busily chewing long tunnels through wood, they don't eat the wood itself. Instead, like fire ants, they have a varied diet. They eat insects and seeds or suck the juices from rotting fruit, vegetables, or flowers.

Other ants, known as harvester ants, live up to their name by gathering or harvesting seeds. They carefully fill special storerooms in their nests with great quantities of seeds. Then they actually grind and crush the seeds with their large, strong jaws. All this chewing results in a powdery food that nourishes all the ants in the colony.

Sometimes the seeds start to sprout before they can be chewed. These thrifty ants quickly carry them outside the mound and leave them to grow. In time the plants will provide the ants with a handy supply of seeds. No wonder they're called harvester ants!

## Living Honeypots

Perhaps the strangest food habits of all can be found among the honey ants. These ants live in the dry plains and deserts of the western United States. Like many ants, their diet is made up of honeydew from other insects; from *nectar,* or the sweet liquid from flowers; and from other plant juices. But unlike many ants, they often have dry desert conditions to contend with, and food isn't always available.

In preparation for the lean times, honey ants store food in a most unusual way. Believe it or not, some worker ants in the colony actually become containers for extra food! When times are good, these ants are fed until they can barely move. Then they hang from the ceiling of the nest until they're needed. In dry periods, they're tapped for food to keep the colony alive. Basically, they're living honeypots!

## Ant Against Ant

An ant's most worrisome enemies often are other ants. Fierce battles sometimes break out between neighboring colonies or different kinds of ants. Most of the large ant battles occur in southern ant colonies. For some reason, northern ants are less aggressive.

What do ants fight about? Are they defending their nests? Or are they protecting the surrounding territory, which they need for gathering food? Whatever the reason, thousands of worker ants will fight for hours—tumbling, biting, and pulling at each other. New ant reinforcements find the battle-grounds quickly by following scent trails. But strangely enough, only a few ants get hurt or killed during these scuffles.

Apart from these battles, some ants are actually hunted, killed, and eaten by other ants.

*Workers called soldiers defend their nest against raiding ants from other colonies.*

Opposite page:
*Ants regularly use their tongue to lick themselves clean.*

## Watch Out, Ants!

It goes without saying that many lizards, birds, and insect-eating mammals have their fill of ants each year. But there's one particularly crafty enemy that ants have to be especially wary of. It's the antlion.

Don't let the name fool you! The antlion is neither an ant nor a lion. It's an insect that looks very much like a small dragon. When this insect is in its larval stage, it burrows into the soil, making a steep-sided pit as it goes. Finally it is completely covered except for its jaws, which poke up through the sand in the bottom of the pit. Here it waits until an ant or other insect falls in and provides it with an easy and tasty snack!

Another ant predator is the tiger beetle. It uses much the same tactics as the antlion. But instead of waiting for the ant to fall into a pit, the tiger beetle leaps out of its hole in the ground like a jack-in-the-box. The ant is then hauled back into the burrow.

# Ants on Guard

All ants are fiercely protective of their colony, and they'll willingly die to defend their queen. The main defense of most ants is their bite. But many, like the fire ant, have a bite that comes with a painful sting, too.

Other ants, such as wood ants, can shoot a bad smelling liquid at attackers, much the way a skunk does. This stinky spray is enough to discourage some animals from making a meal of wood ants!

*Not only are ants hard working; they're also fast. If this creature were the size of a human—but still had its ant speed—it could run five times faster than a champion track star!*

## Thank You, Ants

Some people consider ants a bother. After all, some of them bite, don't they? And they can be annoying at picnics—right? And their appetite for plants can even harm some farmers' crops. But ants have good points, too.

For one thing, they show how well things can work if everyone cooperates. For another, they're fascinating and fun to watch. But most importantly, they help improve the soil by tunneling through it. They break down dead plant material and add air to the soil. This is like having a free gardening service from coast to coast. So the next time you see one of these amazing little ants—don't stand in its way. It has a big job to do!

# Words To Know

**Abdomen**   The tail section of an insect's body.

**Antennae**   The feelers attached to an ant's head. The singular of antennae is *antenna*.

**Caste**   The grouping of ants according to the function they have in the colony.

**Chitin**   The hard material that forms an ant's exoskeleton.

**Cocoon**   The covering of the ant pupa inside of which it develops into an adult.

**Colony**   A group of ants led by a queen.

**Crop**   The part of an ant's stomach where it stores food that is to be used by the other members of the colony.

**Exoskeleton**   The hard outer covering of an ant's body.

**Fungus**   A kind of mushroom.

**Larva**   The second stage in an ant's life after it has hatched from the egg. The plural of larva is *larvae*.

**Mandibles**   The jaw-like parts at the edges of an ant's mouth, used for biting and holding food and other objects.

**Mate**   To come together to produce young.

**Metamorphosis**   The process of changing from an egg to an adult ant.

**Nectar**   The sweet liquid produced by plants.

**Pheromones**   Special chemicals that ants and other animals produce.

**Pupa**   The stage of the ant's life when it is in its cocoon. The plural of pupa is *pupae*.

**Spiracles**   Small holes along the sides of an ant's body through which it takes in air.

**Thorax**   The mid-section of an insect's body.

# Index

PHOTO CREDITS
**Cover:** Bill Ivy. **Interiors:** *Ivy Images:* Bill Beatty, 4, 7; Thomas C. Boyden, 14, 34, 37; Lynn Rogers, 25. /Bill Ivy, 10-11, 13, 26, 29, 31, 32, 40, 43, 44. /*Visuals Unlimited:* Glenn Oliver, 18.